1812 OVERTURE
Op. 49

Peter Ilyitch
TCHAIKOVSKY

DOVER PUBLICATIONS, INC.
Mineola, New York

Copyright

Copyright © 2003 by Dover Publications, Inc.
All rights reserved.

Bibliographical Note

This Dover edition, first published in 2003, is an unabridged republication of the work originally published by Ernst Eulenburg, Leipzig, n.d., as *1812 / Ouverture Solennelle für grosses Orchester / Komponiert zur Einweihung der Erlöserkirche zu Moskau von Peter J. Tschaikowsky / Op. 49 / Komponiert 1880*. Contents and instrumentation pages are newly added.

International Standard Book Number
ISBN-13: 978-0-486-42856-7
ISBN-10: 0-486-42856-7

Manufactured in the United States by Courier Corporation
42856703
www.doverpublications.com

1812

P.I. Tchaikovsky
(1840–1893)
Op. 49

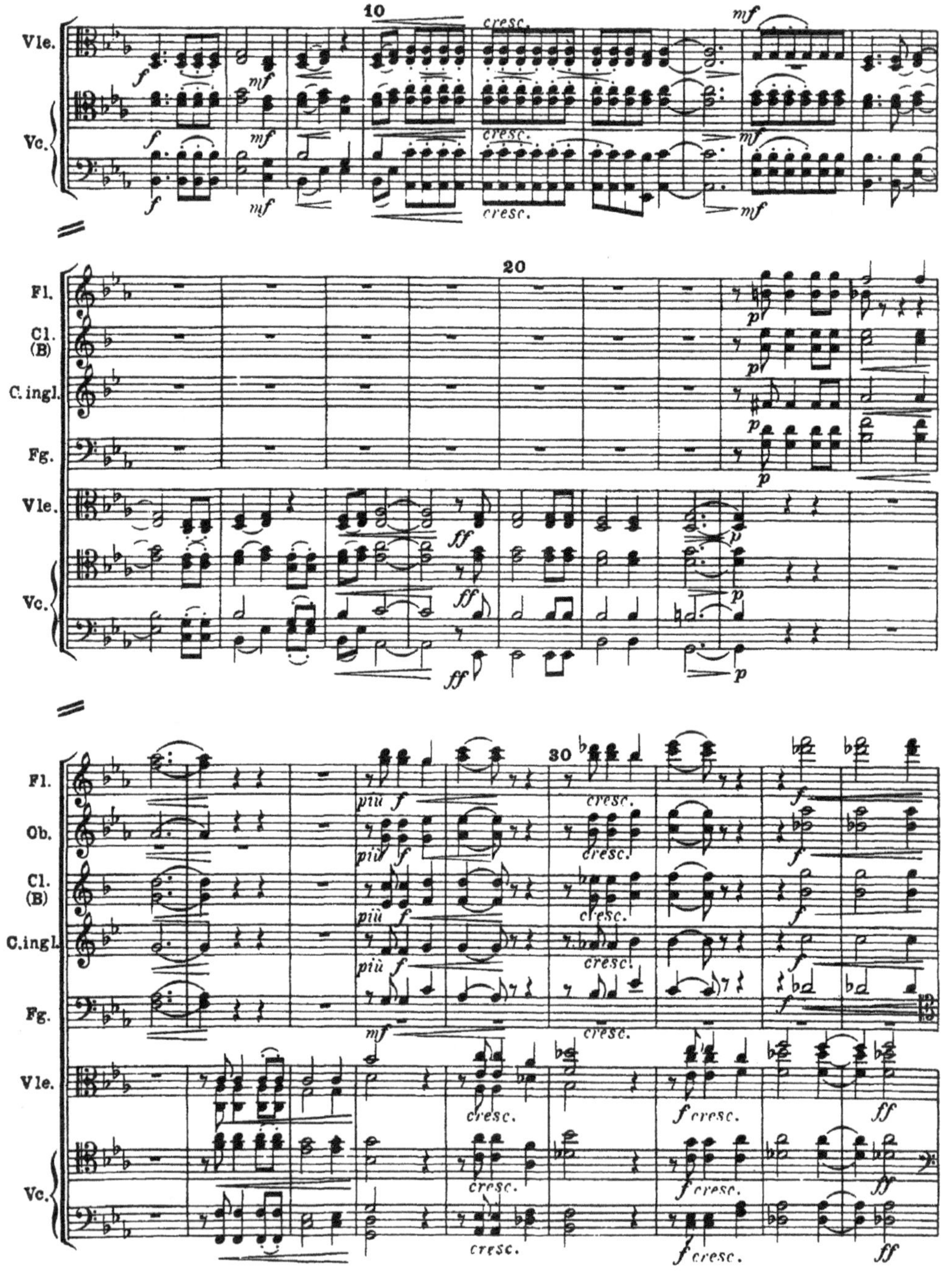
10
cresc.
mf
Vle.
f
mf
Vc.
f
mf
cresc.
mf
f
mf
cresc.
mf
20
Fl.
p
Cl. (B)
p
C. ingl.
p
Fg.
p
Vle.
ff
p
Vc.
ff
p
ff
p
30
Fl.
più f
cresc.
f
Ob.
più f
cresc.
f
Cl. (B)
più f
cresc.
f
C.ingl.
più f
cresc.
f
Fg.
mf
cresc.
f
Vle.
cresc.
f cresc.
ff
Vc.
cresc.
f cresc.
ff
cresc.
f cresc.
ff

Poco più mosso.

10

17

19

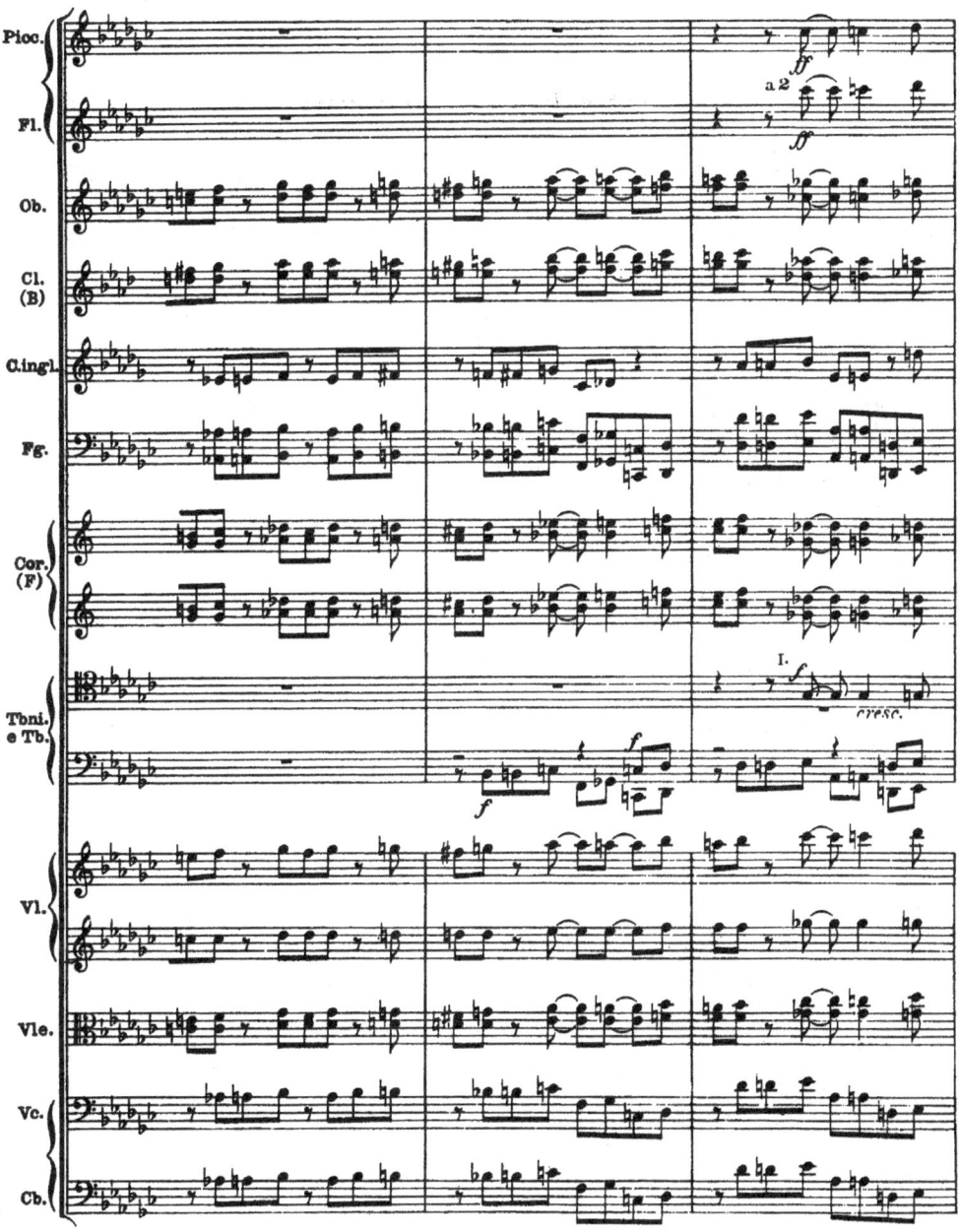

22

26

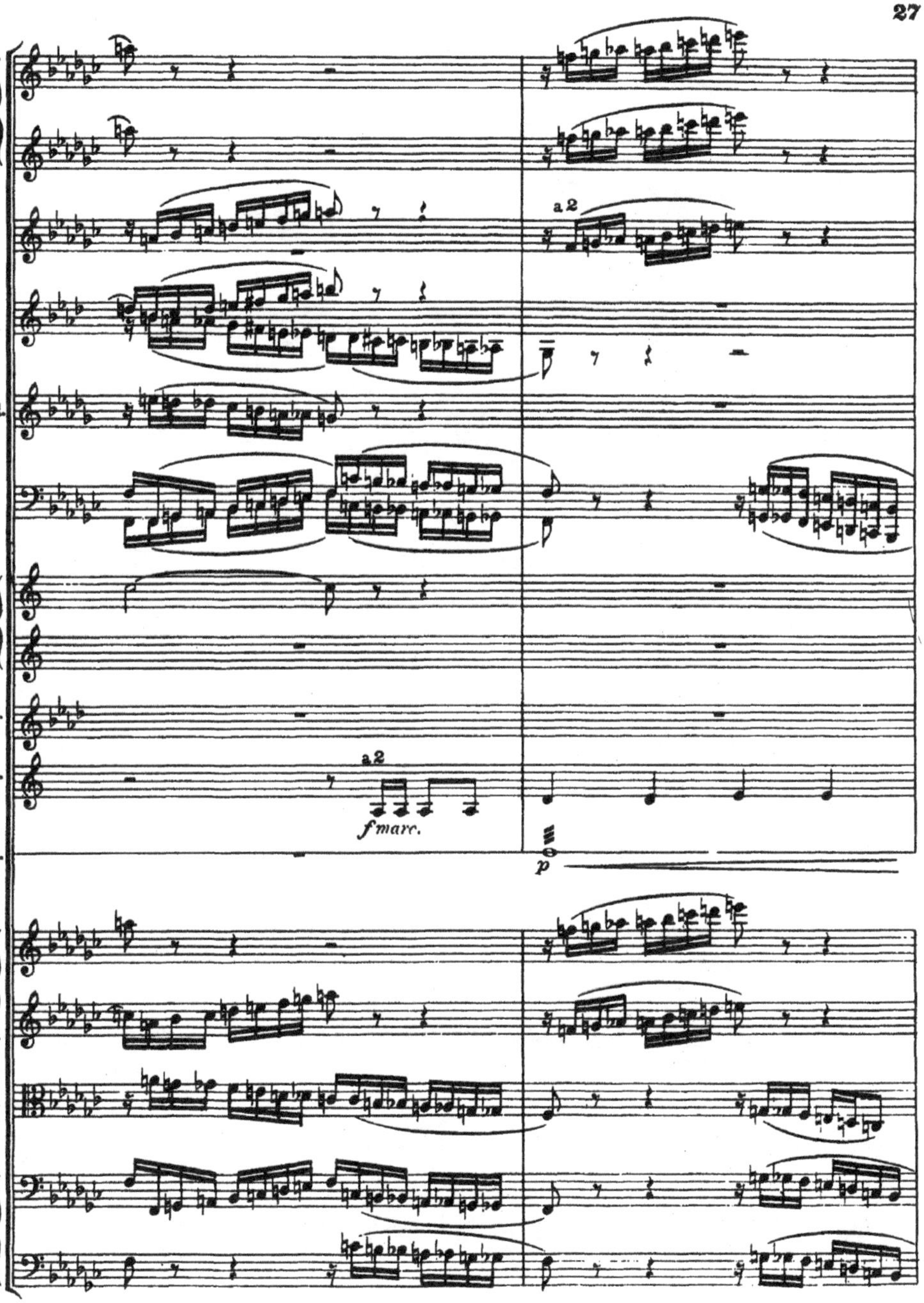
Fl.
Ob.
a 2
Cl. (B)
C.ingl.
Fg.
Cor. (F)
Pist. (B)
Tbe. (Es)
a 2
f marc.
Tb.m.
p
Vl.
Vle.
Vc.
Cb.

28

30

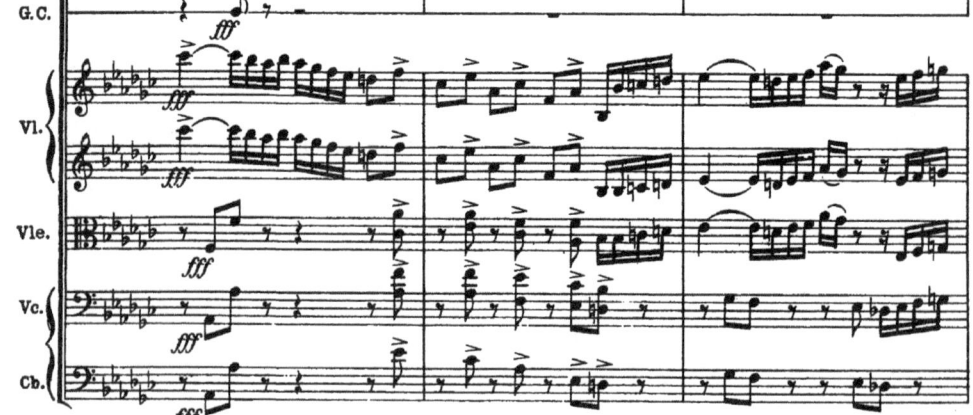

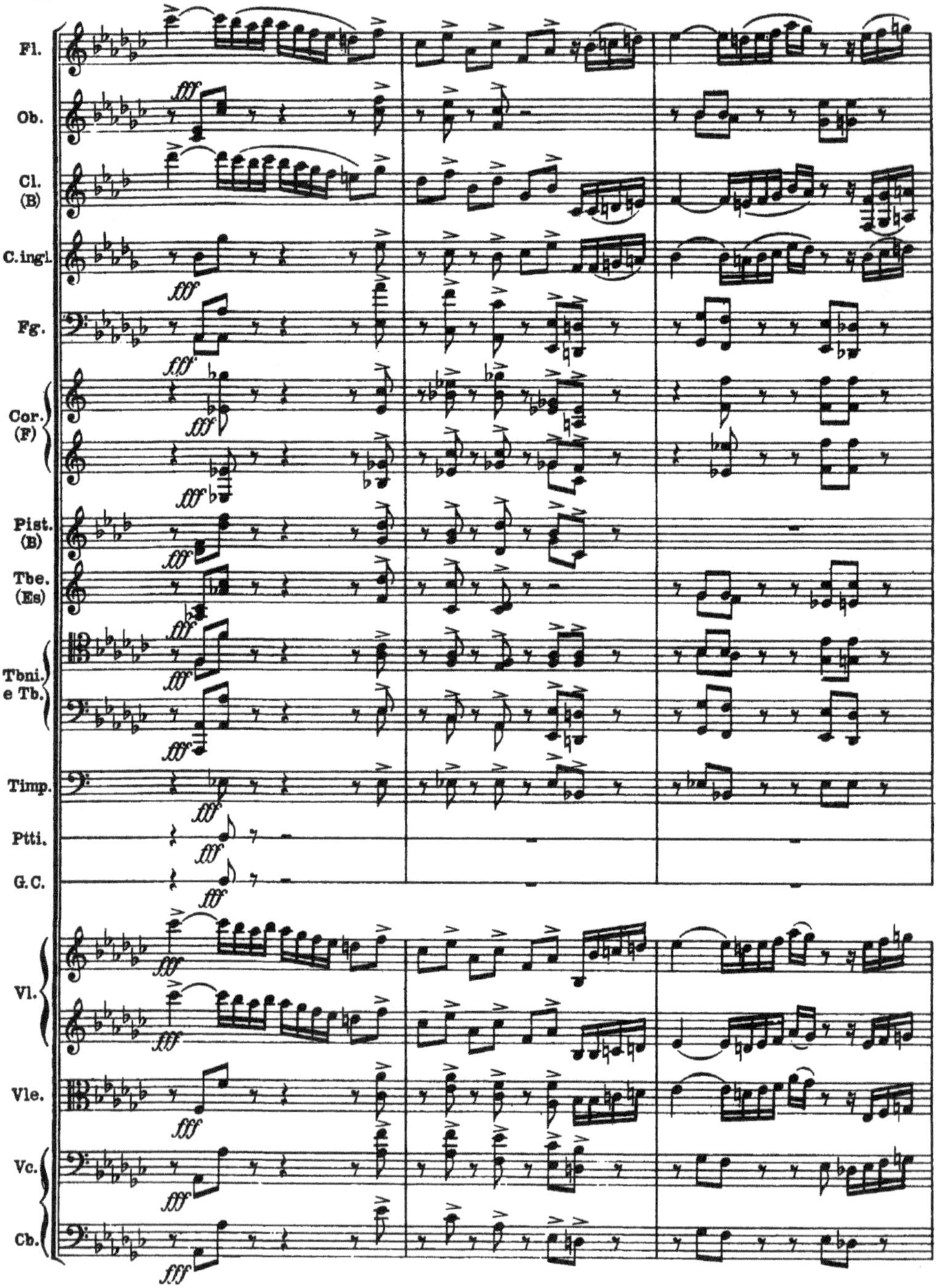
Fl.
Ob.
Cl. (B)
C. ingl.
Fg.
Cor. (F)
Pist. (B)
Tbe. (Es)
Tbni. e Tb.
Timp.
Ptti.
G. C.
Vl.
Vle.
Vc.
Cb.
fff

38

40

42

44

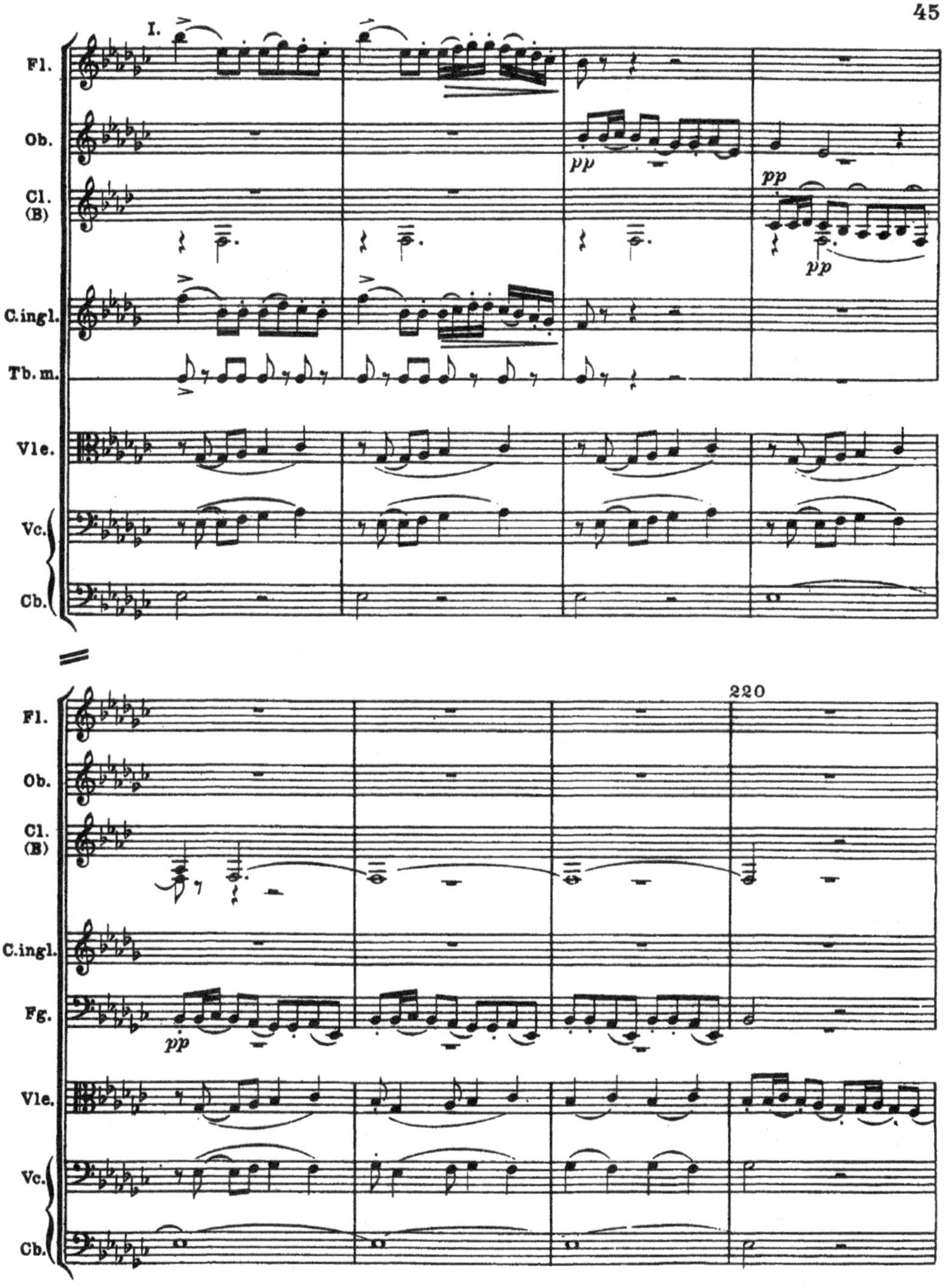
I.
Fl.
Ob.
pp
Cl. (B)
pp
pp
C.ingl.
Tb. m.
Vle.
Vc.
Cb.
220
Fl.
Ob.
Cl. (B)
C.ingl.
Fg.
pp
Vle.
Vc.
Cb.

46

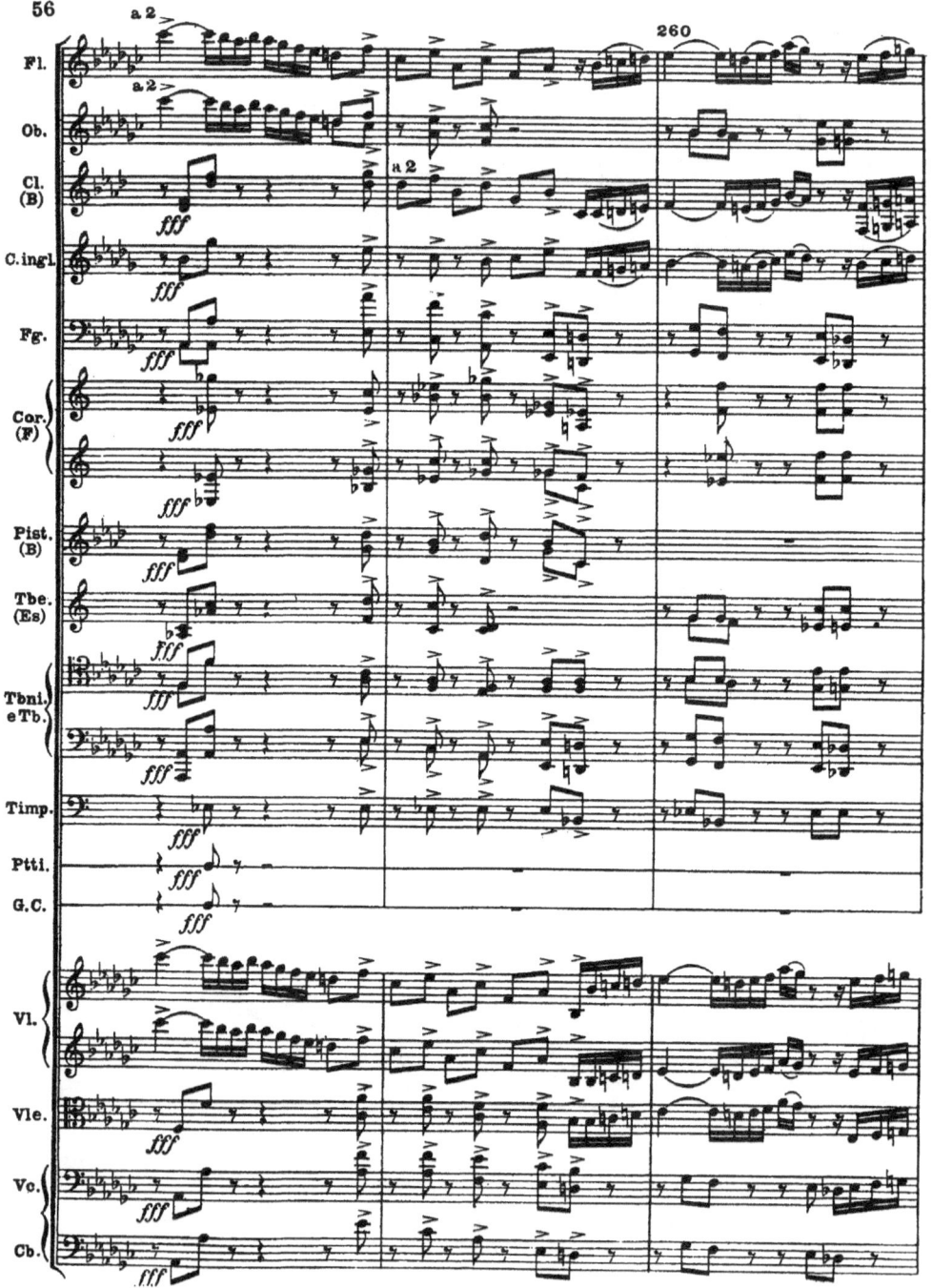

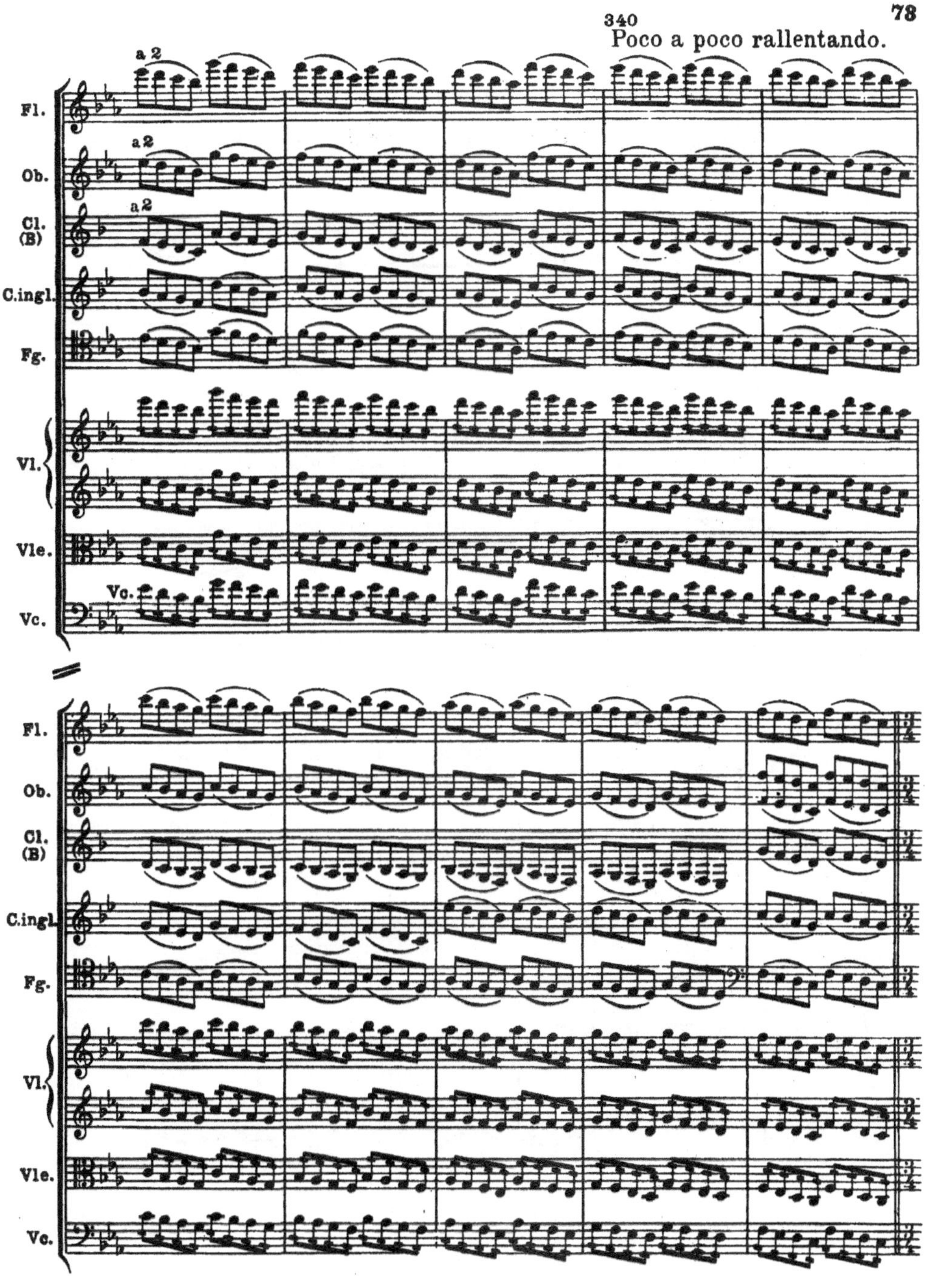
340
Poco a poco rallentando.
a 2
Fl.
a 2
Ob.
a 2
Cl. (B)
C.ingl.
Fg.
Vl.
Vle.
Vc.
Vc.
Fl.
Ob.
Cl. (B)
C.ingl.
Fg.
Vl.
Vle.
Vc.

74

Allegro vivace.

84

87